The Family Kitchen

poems by

Joan Michelson

Finishing Line Press
Georgetown, Kentucky

The Family Kitchen

for my family Glickman and Michelson

Copyright © 2018 by Joan Michelson
ISBN 978-1-63534-398-4 First Edition
All rights reserved under International and Pan-American Copyright Conventions. No part of this book may be reproduced in any manner whatsoever without written permission from the publisher, except in the case of brief quotations embodied in critical articles and reviews.

ACKNOWLEDGMENTS

Some of these poems or earlier versions of them have been published:

Constellations anthology: 'Love Song for My Father'
Liquorish Fish anthology: 'A Kind of Singing'
The Poetry Society UK: 'Self-Portrait with Secret'
Prosopisia International Journal of Poetry and Creative Writing: 'A Kind of Singing', 'Afterword'
Stand Magazine: 'Great Aunt Hero'
Under the Radar 'Love Song for My Father'
Write to Be Counted anthology: 'Great Aunt Hero'

'Storyteller' won first prize in the Bristol Poetry Competition, 2014
'Self-Portrait with Secret' short listed for Poetry Society UK Stanza Prize, 2017

I am grateful to my readers Caroline Brothers, Nelica La Gro, Marina Sanchez, Caroline Stone, Saul Reichlin, Jessica Rosner and Jessica Adkins-Michelson, to proof-reader Jacki Reason and for writing residencies at the Virginia Center for the Arts; OMI International Arts Center; Sangam House, India; and Jentel Artist Residency.

Publisher: Leah Maines
Editor: Christen Kincaid
Cover Art: Jessica Rosner
Author Photo: © photo by John Alexander
Cover Design: Elizabeth Maines McCleavy

Printed in the USA on acid-free paper.
Order online: www.finishinglinepress.com
also available on amazon.com

Author inquiries and mail orders:
Finishing Line Press
P. O. Box 1626
Georgetown, Kentucky 40324
U. S. A.

Contents

The Old Country 1

Legacy 2
Williams Pear 3
Apron 4
Crown of Hair 5
Grandpa from Russia 6
The Business 7
Cousin from Poland 8
Great Aunt Hero 9
Gravestone 10

The New World 11

Full of Years 12
Duck and Cover, 1950s 13
Honeymooners 14
Father the Storyteller 17
Mother the Storyteller 20
Self-Portrait with Secret 21
Hospice Time 22
A Gift of Going 23
Love Song For My Father 30
Reading 31
Afterword 32
The Family Kitchen 33

THE OLD COUNTRY

'and begat
Malka
who begat
Fanny
who begat
Dorothy
who begat
Joan
who begat
.....'

Legacy

They left with little.
My mother said,
'a sack of feathers'.
Yet they brought treasure:
tales untold and told.
This was the family silver,
copper, nickel, pyrite gold.

Williams Pear

The pear that nestled in my grandma's dresser drawer
to ripen for relief of her constipation glimmers

like the goblet that she saw her father bless and lower
to touch it to her mother's fevered lips before she died.

The child that was my grandma saw, or so it's told,
the wedding goblet, which was crystal, struck with light,

a sign that God had sanctified her mother's death.
My mother, who didn't believe in the Old God,

told this story squinting as if she saw the light
I imagine pouring through my kitchen window here

in London. It bathes the pear I bought this morning,
which is standing on my pinewood table glowing.

The pear is ripe. I close my eyes, breathe in sweetness.

Apron

In service to rich cousins in Nova Scotia,
where her father sent her, a twelve year old,
grandma wore a frilly embroidered apron.
Ten years later, for her kosher butcher shop,
she bought a butcher's bib in navy linen.
Sundays when we were small and arrived
for her chicken *tzimmis*[1], she wore a floral print
half-apron, pockets packed with Kleenex tissues,
these for us, nearly twenty-three babies born
in the post-war era. On those Sundays,
her apartment was a *balagan*[2]. Laughing,
she led us round the tables in a skip-step
with her half-apron fluttering.

[1] Yiddish/Hebrew   traditional sweet stew
[2] Yiddish/Hebrew/Russian   chaos

Crown of Hair

She wore a ring of braided chestnut hair
from years before we came into the world,
a Sunday dress for Sunday guests and black
dancer lace-up shoes that shone and tapped.

Most of all she loved to dance, a baby held
against each shoulder, my handsome father
as her partner. Hands on her waist,
he danced her round. Round my grandma went.

Once, her hairpins slipped. Her ring of hair
came loose. It fell across her face and we saw
the grey that lay beneath the crowning brown.

Grandpa from Russia

He escaped call up for the Czar's army,
landed in Massachusetts, took up peddling,
sold what he could carry, cloth and clobber,
and married grandma, although she loved another,
because her father preferred a Hebrew scholar.

Despite her secret heart, she was blessed
with children and came to love grandpa.
They stand together staring at the camera,
a buxom woman and a small, sharp-featured man
clean-shaven in glasses. He lets her take care

of business. To us, grandpa was always distant.
He was busy with the papers, which he read
in Yiddish and in English, or shouting
from a soapbox on the Boston Common,
or holed up in a meeting with his cronies.

He railed against McCarthy and his hunt
for commies. Too hot for us, although my father
and some siblings shared his leanings, grandpa
became a family burden. Finally we put him
on a plane to Tel Aviv to join his brother.

When he came home, it was another era,
the liberated sixties. Now we found him
talking to himself out loud in Russian
-Yiddish. Rigid with resistance and lost,
he shouted, shook and wept.

The Business

In a *shtetl* village
outside of Vilnius,
grandma's mother
kept a tavern.
A young mother
in Massachusetts,
grandma opened
a kosher butcher's.
After meat, she tried
an ice cream parlour.
In the Depression era,
she changed to furniture
with a pickup truck,
which the boys drove,
selling beds for IOUs.
Post-war, a string
of cash-and-carry stores.
Grandpa had a desk.
But she was manager.
The sons were partners,
the daughters, helpers
–resentful yet forgiving
of a woman who'd worked
to educate her children,
and when time came,
to leave a sum for each.
But her dollar stash,
and the house (sold fast),
went on her nursing care.
The boys divvied up
her business share.
The girls went to court.

Cousin from Poland

Berek came to us as a Camp Survivor
and made a life outside of Greater Boston.

He visited my mother shortly before she died.
By then she was, as he mumbled, 'skeletal'.

After we'd buried her and were at home,
sitting around the kitchen table, burdened

with unwanted food, as if his silence
had been broken, Berek spoke of Auschwitz.

He'd been lucky, raised his hand for baker
and landed an outside job. Leaving work,

he'd hidden a long loaf in his pyjama leg.
Now he couldn't imagine how he'd done it.

He'd kept his place and kept in step
marching through the iron gate.

Great Aunt Hero

Great Aunt Hero, whom we never met,
was a rebel and a bundle of lost
letters rumoured to be wonder-epics.

She travelled from Boston, Massachusetts
to San Francisco, to the wilds of China,
to Moscow, Dresden, Honolulu and Oahu.

On Oahu she married a Catholic native,
although she had been born a Jew,
which her six children never knew;

nor the story of her abrupt departure:
locked out by her father (who loved her)
for a misdemeanour with her suitor.

This happened about the time she bobbed her hair,
sent her mother to night school, and heady
with the Bolshevik success, joined the Party,

which she subsequently left. A photo
shows her standing on a piano bench
leading the family orchestra. She holds

her baton high, so high I feel the distance
in her power. Now she rises, rare
as a supernova. She releases waves,

begets bright stars.

Gravestone

Nine hundred years of *shtetl* life wiped out
(and here I am)
in my great-grandmother's village
(more a hamlet)
where she lies buried in a section set aside
(Eternal House)
for the many who died while giving birth.
Six years old
my grandmother witnessed life-in-death
and cradled her baby brother.
My grandmother told her mother's story to my mother.
I write it here
for my granddaughters and their daughters.
Instilled with hate for Jews, someone, maybe soldiers, wrecked
the black basalt headstone that was engraved
(died giving birth)
with a dove rising from a chick-filled nest.

The New World

'my lamp beside the golden door'
The *New Colossus*, Emma Lazarus, 1883

Full of Years

I touch the bark, step back,
look up and see the fork
that's grown high, high.
And see, though far below
and small, the girl I was
so long ago. So high
my perch, my reading nook,
my mother's calling voice.

Duck and Cover, 1950s

When the siren sounded, we tumbled
from our desks to crouch like frogs.

Knees-bent, chins-tucked, our hands
clasped behind our heads, we shrank

between the iron legs and breathed
the sharp smell of dusting powder

swept across the floor boards
by the early morning cleaners.

It was green, as green as grass,
as green as us in this, the era

of our trust. We were a liberal
class, a mix of white, black

and Asian in our coastal Northeast
city with its nineteenth century brick

Elementary school that climbed
four flights of sunken wooden stairs.

Listening for the all-clear signal,
we breathed with care, getting ready

to be the best leaper-up,
the fastest seated, faces lifted

waiting for the next
instruction from our teacher.

Honeymooners

In black and white on my computer screen
a run of moons announces, 'The Honeymooners'.
It's the fifties' sitcom we watched together,
the family and our best friend, Sukey,
who lived next door and came in her pyjamas.

Here's the picture: a small room, a double bed
sagging in the middle, a window shaded
with a yellow Woolworth's blind, a dresser,
and our prized possession—a family gift,
which came with its own magnifying glass,

—a 7" TV. We bunched up for the show.
Drumroll, cymbals, shower of sparks, then violins
with moons, a name on each, rising up
from New York City. Our sitcom was a threat
to Hollywood. It was New York based

with heroes from Brooklyn who are working class.
Ralph drives a bus. Ed works in sewage.
Their wives wear pocket aprons and pinch pennies.
They're masters at making faces, especially Ralph,
played by Jackie Gleason. We competed

working on imitations to be the funniest.
The set is basic: a two-room Brooklyn walk up,
a sink, an ice box, a table covered with a cloth,
a single window with iron bars like prison,
a fire escape, a toilet flushing from the hall.

Ralph comes home, face lit with an idea,
another way to strike it rich. Supper ready,
untying her apron, Alice listens, thinking,
seeing this scheme's flaw. Our mother sees it
just as fast and her wit is just as quick.

But we are busy shouting our own start.
'Hi, Honey. We're getting loads of money.'
'Hi, Honey. Sit down. Supper's ready.'
'Don't tell me what to do. Tell me whatyathink?'
Then we let our mother speak for Alice.

This sets father off and we go with him.
We blow our foghorn noses, wipe our eyes
and school age girls, 6,8,8,9, in shrieking
giggles push each other to the bed-edge.
Here let me pause to wallow in our laughter.

We're not Kramdens who are childless
but we have our own Ralph and Alice.
Our mother knows our father and the world.
Like Alice, she's trim. Like Ralph, he's bulk.
And he too comes up with crackpot schemes.

Our mother lets him dream but like Alice
she's sick of junk. Alice wants Ralph's
family furniture gone. My mother wants
the dishes from the wedding gone. And now
we've inherited an out-of-date TV

from father's brother. And on to father's father
and his Gold Rush scheme. 'Did he find his pot
in California? You bet your boots, he didn't.
He met a blizzard in one of those cold states,
a Dakota. Lost his wagon in a snowstorm.

And picked up Sophia, a girl not yet sixteen.
What kind of screwball guy? He was twenty one!
Brought her home to Boston without a penny,
already one baby. Before you know it, five.
You tell me, Mr Elmer Kramden. What kind of life?'

Was it then my mother pointed out
Ralph and Alice didn't make any babies.
Childless couples could hide a sadness.
On the other hand, a woman might choose
a different way to live her life.

I hear my mother's voice from long ago.
I hear her laugh. I see the scene I'm in
inside the screen, inside the Gleason show,
'The Honeymooners' in a YouTube video,
which I could be watching with the family

if now was then and they were here alive.
It's not a moment for me to count the dead.
My mother knew she would live on in me.
She always said, 'It's okay to live alone.'
It's evening. I am alone. And it's okay.

I watch another episode of 'The Honeymooners'.
It's familiar like family. And another.
Each starts with fireworks and the moon
that comes to life with Gleason's face, his eyes
that bulge, his cheeks like little hills, his grin.

The close up, as large as life, quivers
with a delirium I feel again.

Father the Storyteller

i.

It is always the 1920s in the Jewish ghetto
around Blue Hill Avenue, a day without weather

or season, or other children. My father,
the street storyteller, is six years old.

He dresses up in his mother's clothes,
her cloche, her red fox fur, her bag, her boots.

Like Pinocchio, he forgets to go to school.
In summer he wanders off to L-Street Beach.

Through a crack in the board fence, he watches
his mother chattering, her legs stuck out, reddening.

His sisters, old enough to be his mother,
have gone to work; his brothers, old enough

to be his father, to college. His friend
is the police. They have him sharpen pencils

and draw pictures until his sisters collect him,
or his breathless mother, as happens sometimes.

For the telling, my father keeps changing roles.
He is a little boy, the police, and his mother.

His voice rises high for her distress. 'Help!
My little boy is lost. Can you find him?'

For the police, my father's voice turns gruff.
'Certainly, Madame Mother, we will do our best.'

He pretends Madame mother doesn't recognise
her little boy. He throws his costume off

and throw his arms around himself and cries
in child-voice, 'Mummy, I'm right here.'

ii.

For the new century and his birthday,
his eightieth, we set off for Forty Steps,

the cove at the tip of the Nahant peninsula
which was our haunt. Down the narrow steps

and up the bank of granite boulders to dive
into the breakers. In later years, looking out

he'd made his peace with distance. He'd named
the North Atlantic a bridge between us bringing

England closer. The car long gone, we'd take
the train, walk the mile to the peninsula

and along its length to Forty Steps.
But this journey ended on a wooden bench

where the spit of land began. He sat down heavily,
leaned hard against me and told a story

rich with pity. The summer he was five,
his mother left him in Uncle Lenny's cottage,

a rental for the month of August. On weekends,
Uncle Lenny came up from Boston to go fishing.

The cousins, Milt and Harry, were young men
always tinkering with their car. Aunt Gert

fed him and forgot him. He gestured
at the cottages and let his arm fall back,

hand open as if to show the emptiness he'd felt
and felt. Which day was I flying to England?

He knew I had to go and that we die alone.
Yet I felt accused of abandoning the child

in the worn out man. In this telling
he'd resorted to melancholy self-exposure,

no drama, no laughter, none of his teasing
playful manner that was so endearing.

We were saved by the Nahant police.
On duty, slowly driving round, one checked us out.

My father asked him which way he was headed.
With the police, a transformation.

He was the story-teller child, lost, found
and taken to the station to his friends.

They wanted stories. Our day was now adventure.
We'd seen England across the water and met

a young policeman so considerate,
he drove us to our train and right on time.

Mother the Storyteller

Her stories kept childhood alive.
Even dying, her face lit up.
Imagine it. She has the story.
Off we go in the Ford jalopy.

Today it's wild-coloured autumn.
Today the trip's for women only.
We take my grandma, aunts, a cousin,
and my mother's blind Aunt Elsa.

Up the steep mountain road,
up to the Tiptop House.
But will the Old Ford make it?
It creaks. It weeps. It shrieks the brakes.

I bounce the bed to be the car.
I eeee for wind that rocks the trees.
I knock for limbs to bring down leaves
in heaps. When the T breaks down

completely, we're at the treeline.
Stands of stunted fir and spruce.
Mats of prostrate fir and spruce.
Above us, hulking granite boulders

from the long ago Ice Age.
The family spills out like circus folk,
the dead, alive and the yet alive.
My mother and I watch our loved ones

straggling down the road. They bed
in layered leaves on mattresses
of needles fallen from mixed pines.
We whisper, as we leave the story.

Sleep, my dear ones. Sleep and wake.

Self-Portrait with Secret

i.
This could be the outer door.
It's heavy and hard to open.
Behind it, another, and mother,
an absence I cannot enter.

She came home at the end
of summer. The brightness. Scent
of lavender. I am running, longing
to embrace my mother.

ii.
Six weeks. Two foster homes.
I share a bed with my younger sister.
She holds my hand to sleep and wets
the bottom sheet. No one scolds.

But in early August, my father
quits his job to bring us home.
At the end of summer, he signed
for mother. She looked small, smaller.

iii.
Sometimes I can almost reach her.
Sometimes I can run without
stopping. The light. Her lavender.
Waking to the world, I face

my first day of school. Mother,
away since winter, goes on sitting,
in the yard-chair, her face pale
and lifted towards the sun.

Hospice Days

She was excited. She was getting a new bed.
But it was a giant crib with wide-set bars.

One day we found her fallen to the floor,
—unbroken, her good eye open like a bird's.

Tucked back in, she tipped her head and winked.
In mock protest, she said, 'I am not

having another baby.' We smiled gently.
We lifted her from bath to bed, kept her

warm in flannel nighties, empire beauties
with silky ribbon threaded through the wrists.

She liked the pink bows she saw and how
the ribbon felt against the cheek that God

had left unblemished so one side was pure.
When a bow came loose, she tried to tie it.

Long she tried before she offered us her cuff.
'You girls can do it for me just this once.'

A Gift of Going

Twenty years I've let this lie
and still her whispering high-pitched nasal...
Although there was an end, her mouth
open like a beak on empty.

i.
Dear Mother,
We argue as if you have not gone.

Dear Heart of my Mother,
As if you still beat.

Nose of my Mother,
As if you drip forever,
since the doctor fixed 'The Jewish'.

Dear Boney Knuckled Fist
that dabs her handkerchief at drips.
which she insists are mostly water.

And Green-Flecked-Eye
that's buried beneath her scabby cheek
that leaks as if it sees within and weeps.

ii.
'How can it be water, mother?'
You raise your pointer finger.
'It's connected.'

Scientific fact:
The human body and the earth
are two-thirds water.

Tonsil tale:
'They sat me in a kitchen chair.
The doctor came and knocked me out.
I woke and spat out blood like crazy,
but it wasn't blood really.'

Postpartum trick:
I didn't have a clue what hit me.
I thought it was another baby.
'The Holy Mary After-Baby,
that was blood really.'

Saga:
You fell so ill, you felt so low,
you did not want to talk to dad.

Your sister let you stay the night.
But in the morning—on the bus.

Dad's brother took you in his car.
Dad went along to sign you in.

Insulin that made you fat and dozy.
ECT for jaw ache and the woozies.

'They needed guinea pigs, I guess,'
you say, 'for their experiments.'

And when you hid beneath the bed
because of lightning storms with claps,

they locked you in a padded cell
and kept you talking to yourself.

iii
Now you're dying and you argue.
'Listen to your mother. Water.'

You touch the lump that is a tumour.
'Gosh, I must have bumped my head.'

Then you tell us what you'll do
when this has ended and you're better.

iv
'I've been away,' you say to me.
'I've been to hell and I've come back.

They made me walk across the North Atlantic.'
You pause for effect.

'Carrying a rocket on my head.'
You add, 'For John Glenn, I guess.

They made him circle round the earth
standing on his head and bouncing.'

You quick-change, dead-pan face,
then laugh at your own twist of thought.

Your next words stop my heart.
'Joan, can you hear music?'

'Joan,' you say, 'My birds are singing.
When you hear music you don't want to die.'

You smile as if with secret joy.
and turn your head from side to side.

I see the glints in your good eye.
Then snarling squint. Your blanket's red.

The bloody baby mary red
immaculate conception jesus
on the radio it's christmas carols
keeping god too busy

'Red,' you shout. 'Joan, get it out.'
I sack your Bloody Baby rage

in a plastic kitchen bag that's black.

'Okay,' you say, 'we can enjoy our soup.
You tell your father to bring soup.'

Dad brings you bloody beef tomato.
'Red!' you shout, 'Joan, get it out.'

From calm to rage to calm again.
And then an adage from Ben Franklin

which you adapt. 'It's good to rest
my stomach for a day.'

As if each day does not repeat
the fact that you can't eat.

v
I see you shrink like Alice Wonder
eating from the giant mushroom.

You exclaim at blue-sky wonder
in your window. And the hookah.

And Carroll's three-inch caterpillar.
Offended, he said to Alice,

grown so small she matched his size,
'You'll get used to it in time.'

You lift an arm to stare at bone,
you stare at your pale skin and bone.

Which side to eat to make you grow?
You close your eyes as if to see.

As if you know, you smile
like the Cheshire cat.

vi.
The hospice brings a pack of sponges,
mini cubes with toothpick handles.

I squeeze the cubes to feed you droplets,
sponge your thirsty gums and tongue.

vii.
'If she suffocates,' I'm told,
'she won't feel a thing.'

It's not a thought I want to think.
But it's a thought the nurse repeats.

She adds we'll know death's near
when she stays dry.

viii.
You call out to your dead again.
'Ma, I'm coming. Best friend Molly.'

You also call to God. But God can't listen.
He's too busy, hears too many.

singing mary jesus carols
bloody baby poor king wenceslas
cannot stop today for you
must go on waiting god's too busy

ix
Dad comes in. He says your name.
He says, 'I know you want to die.'

You say to him, 'Now you speak
a tiny portion of the truth. For sooth.'

Head bowed, he sits beside your bed.
He tells me mutely, 'I am ready'

x.
Dear Mother,
You sent me out.
Why?
I wanted to stay in.
You told me to go out.
You said you say I hear you say,
'God said, "'Enjoy life."'

xi.

I went out.
I walked the frozen streets.
The lights came on.
You died.
Years passed.
Years pass.
It's summer, winter,
Alice Wonder blue.
Your birds are singing.
Your good eye opens.
I hear your song.

Love Song for My Father

The past falls open anywhere.
You're there. You shut the door and shake.
You shake off snow, your boots, your death.
You're courting mother in the year
before I'm born. The war is on.
Your call up notice in the post.
You shake. You fail the test. You stay

home. And when you're old and talk
returns to war, you speak of love
and birth. Open-mouthed, the joke
on you, you start to laugh. The snow.
The dizzy bliss. Coatless, delirious,
your trousers back-to-front,
you rush out to greet me, just born.

Reading

I wake and see my father reading.
He's sitting in a kitchen chair,
or on the couch that disappeared
the year he moved into The Home.

Or in the chair that eases back
and lifts his legs, gift of M,
who suddenly 'passed'. On his lap
her woollen throw and his.

Spirit now, he's far from me.
But still I see him sitting near.
He's dressed for work or dressed for bed,
shawled and sitting in his chair.

I hear the tick of our old clock
and then the turning of a page.
These hours are mine as they were his.
I read in bed and breathe his breath.

Afterword

In my last years—
maybe I will
build a nest.

Maybe I will build
and sing in the branches
scratching at the window.

If I don't return—
you might make a home
in my room.

Books on the shelves.
A round ceramic lamp.
Words like moths

opening their wings.

The Family Kitchen

I push through a field of grass
grown higher than my head
to reach a clearing.

In it, a new-built house
with a window swinging open
like a door.

I see myself sitting
with my red-haired sister
at a Formica counter.

My father is cooking breakfast.
He wears my mother's apron
which barely fits him.

Dead so much longer,
white in her white nightie,
my mother hovers.

As it might have been:
an embrace of summer
with father cooking pancakes

sweet with crushed berries,
—the wild blues we found
in the near wood.

Joan Michelson completed an MFA at Columbia University, New York, before moving to England. Appointed to a lectureship at the University of Wolverhampton, she developed and directed Creative Writing and Holocaust Studies: Literature. She currently teaches within Medical Humanities at Kings College, London and directs community creative arts projects.

After her husband died in 1997, she turned from writing prose to poetry. Her first full-length collection, *Toward to Heliopause*, Poetic Matrix Press, CA, 2011, is a response to his death and a dialogue between his poems and hers. It was short-listed for the Rubery Book Award, UK. A chapbook, treating a community of residents in an Assisted Living Home, a fictional place informed by visits, *Bloomvale Home* was published by Original Plus Books, Wales, 2016, and in a Romanian-English parallel texts edition by Integral Books, Bucharest, 2017. Her second full collection, *Landing Stage*, a competition prize-winner, treating refugee and immigrant stories, was published by SPM Sentinel Books, Ltd, London, 2017.

Her stories and poems have been selected for anthologies of new writing by both the British Council and the Poetry Society of England. Poems have won first prize in the Bristol Poetry Competition, UK, Torriano International Poetry Competition, UK, and the Poetry Society's Hamish Canham annual members' competition.

She has been a recipient of writing fellowships in the United States and elsewhere including the MacDowell Colony, the Virginia Center for the Arts, OMI International Arts, the Djerassi Foundation, Key West Artists' Studios, Sangam House, India, and Fundación Valparaíso, Spain.

Born in New England, she lives in London, England.

www.ingramcontent.com/pod-product-compliance
Lightning Source LLC
LaVergne TN
LVHW041604070426
835507LV00011B/1299